# The Namaste Garden

**Written and Illustrated by Maria Triano**

*"Plant your dreams and watch them grow"*

Balboa Press books may be ordered through booksellers or by contacting:

Balboa Press
A Division of Hay House
1663 Liberty Drive
Bloomington, IN 47403
www.balboapress.com
844-682-1282

ISBN: 978-1-4525-8764-6 (sc)
ISBN: 978-1-4525-8765-3 (e)

Library of Congress Control Number: 2013921330

Print information available on the last page.

Balboa Press rev. date:  01/04/2022

BALBOA.PRESS
A DIVISION OF HAY HOUSE

# DEDICATION

This book is dedicated to the children of our world, to you, to me, to all of us,
and to All That Is, God, the Divine, the Creator...however you see or connect
to the energy of Love that created us all,
which is making life happen through us, for us, and in us.

The dedication of this book is also to my family
and those whom I've been blessed to teach and inspire through my dance career.

And to my mother, Kathy...
"When you wish upon a star, makes no difference who you are,
anything your heart desires, will come to you." I love you, Momma.
(From the 1940's Walt Disney story of "Pinocchio",
music and lyrics by Leigh Harline and Ned Washington.)

# Acknowledgements

I would like to thank my best friend and husband, Mike Abate, for his understanding, friendship and support through all that needed to occur and take place in my personal excavation process over the years in order to bring a project like this to completion, and honestly, for all of the other projects and creations along the way as well. He helped me in every way he knew how and even in ways he didn't. I love you and am grateful for your presence in my life.

I would also like to acknowledge my 8 year old nephew, Robert Triano III, for being the first person I shared this book with when it was still written on scratch-paper and in pencil. I feel so grateful to have this amazing little boy in my life who was able to 'get it' before he even finished reading it. The joy and delight I felt pouring from his Spirit filled my heart with so much love and happiness.

When my oldest nephew, James, (who is now 24), was 7 years old, I taped his school picture on the inside cover of a book that really inspired me about teaching children; it was called *How To Talk So Kids Can Learn*, by Adele Faber and Elaine Mazlish. The love I felt for my nephew inspired me to be the best Aunt I could be. I also intended to the best teacher I could possibly be to my dance students. I vowed to care about how I was sharing, interacting, and teaching children (especially those in my own family!) and to see each child as their own unique individual. Looking back now to that moment in 1995, I realize that I heard a whisper inside of me say that I would someday write a book myself. I neither agreed nor denied that whisper because until now, I didn't remember hearing it. Wow, what an amazing feeling!

I am also very grateful to my Rebel Road Tour soul-friend, Simran Singh, for writing the beautiful ("Be-you-to-fullness") review you see on the back cover. She did this while literally in the midst of her 66-city tour where she is inspiring people from all over the globe with her inspirational talks and is sharing her new book *Conversations with the Universe* with the world.

Last and certainly, not least…Thank you, Gram! I know you've been guiding me all along.

# A Word From the Author:

While I was practicing a heart-opening meditation, I became cognitively and spiritually aware that we all have our own private sanctuary living inside of us. It is a place where the Higher Self resides. It is a garden; a creative, landscape. A sacred garden where the Higher Self lives, breathes, enjoys the fullness of nature, flows through "doing", in an effortless, unbounded, blissful way. In this state of awareness, the Higher Self is completely healthy in all ways, is always at peace, creates and manifests its dreams, and plants seeds in the soil of Love which blossom into your reality.

It is my hope that you will allow yourself to be transformed by the art, words, messages and energy contained within this book to create magic and miracles in your own life. Share the book and teachings with your children and those you love, so that they can be in constant connection and in a loving relationship with who they really are.

Did you know that everyone has a garden living inside of them?
It's true.
And here's how I know.

One day while I was feeling rather blue,
I closed my eyes, took a long, deep slow breath,
and was led by my Guardian Angel
to a beautiful landscape.

*Can you imagine this?*

*Try it now.*

I could see the rolling hills laid out in front of me
and the smell of the fresh clean air.

Everything was crisp and colorful against the comforting blue sky.

Trees and wild flowers placed just so, even a big glorious pond to enjoy.

This majestic landscape rolled on forever with no end in sight.
And I could see the sun's supportive rays over the peaks and valleys.
It was as if I was larger than this lush landscape somehow.

*What does your landscape look like?*

As I glanced down at myself,
I could even see what I was wearing.
It was my favorite type of clothing.
When I looked at my feet,
I noticed that they were running and dancing, and so too was I.

*Can you see your clothes and feet?*
*What are you wearing?*

The wind in my hair and on my cheeks,
the sun and the sweet blue sky were my friends.
The grass beneath me, so warm and happy to greet me.
I was more than a part of this special place; I belonged to it.

There were no cares or worries
    inside of my beautiful landscape, just nature,
    freedom
        and fun.

Lots of peace and love was everywhere
and in everything, even the air.
That's what it was all made of.
I was even made of it.
Oh, sweet JOY!

As my feet continued to walk,
I noticed I was on a path,
which laid itself out before me;
each piece of the path showing
up for me when I needed it.

Because I was so curious,
I played with my steps...
first walking really fast, then running,
then slowing it way down...
no matter the speed, the path
still showed up for me,
never running out.

*What does your
path look and feel like?*

My path took me to an opening
of a brand new place I'd never been to before.

It was a garden.

My own special garden of magic and love.

No one was allowed there but me.

In a flash, I knew that this garden lived inside of me
and it was where my heart was creating all of its life from...
where my dreams were being planted by no one else but me.
How exciting!

*Can you see into your special garden?*

I danced my way through the garden
to see what was there, when I noticed "her".

Another "me" who was <u>already in the garden.</u>

Wow! Another "me"?

She was a grown up version of me and so beautiful.
I loved everything about her.
I watched as she tended to the garden…
admiring what was growing and what was about to sprout.

*Can you see your grown up self in your garden?*

*Take a moment to look.*

I walked closer to her and looked over her shoulder.
It was like I was inside of her…with myself.
Me. Myself. And I.

All "we" did, was all we wanted to do,
and all we wanted to do was
everything and nothing at all.

*Walk closer now…go ahead…
it's a wonderful feeling.*

We were planting in the magic soil.
She told me I could plant anything my heart desired,
things that I wanted to enjoy in my life…
things I wanted to share with others.
This delighted me and I became excited.
Not only could I plant feelings, but objects too.

*What great things are you ready to plant?*

Kneeling down, I made a spot in the soil where I placed a red, glass heart.
As I covered it up, a watering can appeared just when I needed it.
I watered the soil and then gently waved my hands across it.
Rainbow light and sparkles poured from my hands into the soil.
I knew the light was Love. I was happy.

*Now it's your turn to plant something.*

I stood up and backed away a little to see if something was happening,
when right in front of my eyes it started to grow!
It grew fast and it grew <u>now</u>!
A whole tree sprouted up where sparkling crystals hung on its branches.
The tree told me there was more to come when I visited next…
lots more planting and surprises.

*What did you plant and what sprouted up in your garden?*

Although it all seemed like magic to me,
something about this whole thing seemed very natural and normal.
Somewhere inside of me I knew that time stood still
and that everything happened right now.
I felt so thankful in my heart to know how I was creating things.
I also knew in my heart that everyone else
was doing the same thing, they just didn't know it.

They all had a garden of Love, Light, and Magic living inside of them.
It didn't matter if they were a boy or a girl, what their age,
and it didn't matter what they looked like or
how much money they had.
We all had one...and we were all ONE.

I thought about us all being one as I sat underneath
a fragrant cherry blossom tree nearby.
The flowers from the tree were so inviting and pleasant to be with.
They seemed to hold me while I sat.
They reminded me that I was one with the birds, the stars, the grass, the ocean,
the moon, and the sun…because I was Love, I was in
everything, and everything was in me.
And because you are Love, you are one with everything too.

A big smile filled my face.
My heart opened wide with JOY to meet and greet everyone
and everything in loving kindness.

The word "Namaste" (nama-stay) bubbled up
from my heart and came out of my lips.
I said it out loud, "Namaste".
Ahhh…I was at peace and happy.

I heard a voice inside of me saying,
"I know and believe I am Love.
I know and believe you are too.
I know and believe we are all created from the same Love.
When we are in Love, we are One."
"Namaste."

*Namaste, my dear friend.*

Just then, I gazed out over my garden
and saw an arch forming across the sky, this is what it said.

**"The Namaste Garden"**
**Plant your dreams and watch them grow.**

Wow! What an amazing feeling this is!
I took a deep breath into that awesome feeling and smiled brightly,
lighting up my whole body with happiness and Love.
As I rested in that wondrous feeling for a few moments,
I saw myself standing in the middle of the rainbow
with sparkling light all around me.
It seemed to be going through me too.

*Can you feel that? Can you see that?*

As the colorful energy flowed through every part of me,
I took a fresh, new breath…
Noticing in my mind that my feet
were once again walking back
through The Namaste Garden, along my path,
back to where I came from when
this whole journey began.

*Are you back from your special garden?*
*Wiggle your fingers and toes and take a deep breath*
*into your body now.*
*Wasn't that an amazing journey?*

What a special gift to learn
something about myself and
about everyone else too, I thought.
My life felt different now and I loved myself.
I loved that I could plant my own dreams
and that they would always find a way to come to
life in ways that would surprise and delight me.

I remembered some wisdom the cherry blossom tree shared with me.
It said, "It's fun to see how pieces of your dreams will pop up
when you least expect them and know that they will.
Some time, some place, somewhere, they will all show up just for you.
Make sure to notice."

"You've been planting your dreams long before you
can even remember and you'll never stop.
Expect your dreams to come to you in ways that inspire you to see what's next,
being patient, kind, and loving to yourself and others along the way.
And please visit your garden any time you'd like to plant more or to rest in JOY…
especially before bed, as you drift off to sleep, or upon waking each morning.
It only takes a moment or in the blink of on eye."

From that moment on I felt safe and warm inside of myself.
I began to notice signs and symbols everywhere directing me
to the things I planted in The Namaste Garden.
There were lots of ways these friendly messages would show up…
and they came to support me, help me, guide me, and lead me to my dreams.

Noticing the messages took a bit of practice, which I learned very quickly.
They never stopped showing up and they were delivered
in the simplest of ways, just like the tree said.
They wanted me to find them so they showed up in ways that I could understand.
Sometimes by hearing the words of a song…by noticing
the color and shape of something…
by creating…by writing…by hearing my own thoughts…
by listening to something someone said…by feeling a feeling or an emotion…
by doing a certain activity…by being in nature or even by looking at the clouds.

*Have you ever looked up at the sky and noticed
animals, the ocean, or angels floating by?*

These messages are there all of the time
if I take a moment to notice them.

They were showing me the way...

one step at a time.

Dear You,

*The Namaste Garden* is a real experience I had while meditating with a focus on my heart in January 2013. I was awe-inspired to find a whole life being cultivated and communicated through the window of the open heart where Divine Love lives in us all. As a result, I was guided by God to share this experience with all of you and to serve as a bridge for you to connect to your own Spirit.

*The Namaste Garden* was written initially as a children's book, but after sharing the contents with some of my family members and close friends, I realized this was a book for everyone. It helps us to remember the child within us all who knows the Truth.

By doing the healing work of freeing my true self and learning about the unique Gifts that I was born with, I confidently and lovingly teach others to free themselves and to stay true to themselves as they honor and walk their path through the journey of Life.

I believe that we were all born with special Gifts and Talents. We all have the ability to connect with ourselves in a way that can allow our Spirit's to live freely within the human body, so that we can thoroughly enjoy being alive. I believe in living from the voice of our Spirit's, first, and once the Spirit has been invited to be in the driver's seat of our lives, that we can then begin to follow and take action on our inner-knowingness to create and experience Joy and Bliss. Heaven on Earth. I am blessed and honored to guide, nurture, and teach the path of Oneness, as I walk my own path in the human experience, one step at a time.

Blessings to you as you walk your path.

✻❀ Namaste ❀✻
Maria

# ABOUT THE AUTHOR

Maria Triano is a Lightworker, Reiki Master, Certified Angel Card Reader™, spiritual intuitive and guide, successful and passionate dance, yoga and movement educator, meditation teacher, performer, choreographer, artist, entrepreneur and mentor, who has been sharing her Gifts for over 25 years. In the heart of the Pocono Mountains of Pennsylvania, Maria offers her many programs and private sessions at her studio, PA Dance Network.

Her years of self-exploration and self-discovery led her to a dedicated and focused practice of meditation and energy work. She has been, and continues to be, inspired by many wonderful teachers, authors and dancers whom she's had the privilege of studying with, taking classes with and learning from; they include: Louise Hay, Deepak Chopra, Doreen Virtue, Wayne Dyer, Shakti Gawain, Julia Cameron, Denise Linn, Alvin Ailey, Martha Graham, Jeffery Ferguson, Bob Rizzo, Jiavanna Skolnik, Elizabeth Gibbons, Catherine Culnane, Karen Bishop, Simran Singh, Rebecca Devine, Melanie Beckler and Colette Baron-Reid.

Maria's teachings are fast moving to a full educational hub of live interaction and audio/video learning where you can work with Maria and her team of instructors, receive healing, take movement and meditation classes and learn about yourself online. Her SoulStar Yoga Teacher Training©, Dance for the Joy of it: A Creative Dance Journey-STEPPING STONES© Dance Teacher Training Program, Reiki Trainings, live online class membership packages and one-on-one coaching sessions are all available via the internet and in-person at her studio in PA.

For more information about Maria's work, please send an email to maria@padancenetwork.com or visit her website, www.padancenetwork.com. Like & follow her on Facebook at www.facebook.com/padancenetwork and Instagram @mariatriano882

❋ A SPECIAL GIFT FOR YOU! When you write a book review of The Namaste Garden on amazon.com, you will receive a free emailed Angel guidance message. To receive your email Angel message, read the book, write your review and send an email to Maria at maria@padancenetwork.com letting her know that you have submitted your review and are ready for your Angel message. Responses will be made to you via email within 2 weeks. Thank you and EnJOY! ☙

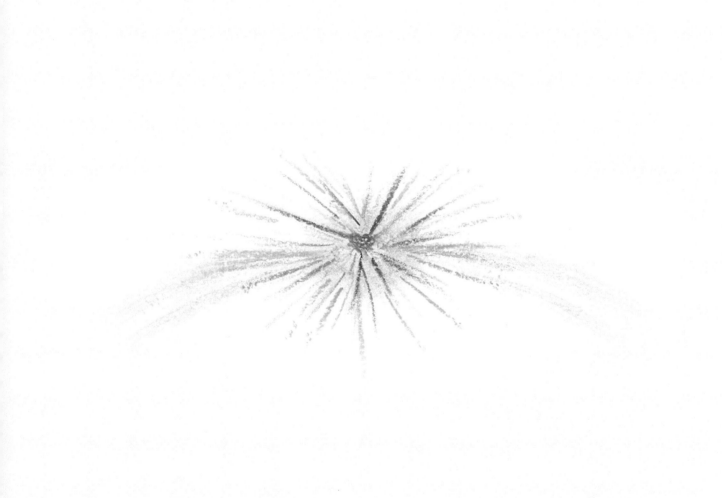

Printed in the United States
by Baker & Taylor Publisher Services